Julia Clements
FLOWER ARRANGING MADE EASY

BROCKHAMPTON PRESS
LONDON

**Also by Julia Clements
and published by Cassell:**

Flower Arranging for All Occasions, 1993

My Life with Flowers, 1993

Julia Clements
FLOWER
ARRANGING
MADE EASY

Cassell Publishers Limited
Wellington House, 125 Strand
London WC2R 0BB

First published 1995

British Library Cataloguing-in-Publication Data
A catalogue record for this book is available from the
British Library

This edition published 1998 by Brockhampton Press.
a member of Hodder Headline PLC Group

ISBN 1 86019 8848

Edited by Anthea Matthison
Designed by Judy Linard
Illustrations by Coral Mula

Typeset by Litho Link Ltd, Welshpool, Powys, Wales

Printed in Dubai

CONTENTS

Introduction

Many of you will wonder why I am going back to the beginning and writing a book on 'how to do it' after having written more than twenty books on every facet of the subject.

I wonder myself also, but my publishers remind me that there are tens of thousands of you out there, who are not members of flower clubs, Women's Institutes or adult education classes, who long to arrange flowers artistically but do not know how to start.

I am also reminded that a new generation has emerged since I wrote my first book who are curious about the queues of visitors round the flower-arrangement tent and the hall at flower shows and festivals. Of course I know that not everyone wants to (what is called) *arrange* their flowers; many like to see them just placed in water. And they are quite right. They may be occupied with other things, just as we do not all want to paint, embroider or cook.

But if you want to see flowers in the home as an expression of yourself, then a few tips on how to effect this will not go amiss. You do not need a lot of time or money. It all depends upon what you want to do: you can make an effective design with five flowers and a branch in a few minutes or a larger design for a special occasion which will take much longer. However, whatever you do, enjoy doing it, set aside half an hour to create a picture, choose your flowers with care and thought and put your heart into it, making it something of your own.

I am often asked why the subject is so popular. I think it is because of that satisfying sense of achievement we all feel when someone notices what we have done. Not everyone has the time to take up painting, music or any other of the expressive arts, but we can all, and I do mean all, take up flower arranging and see the result almost at once. Whether you have a large garden or a small one or none at all, there is always the countryside and the flower shops. It is also the easy accessibility of the basic materials required that makes it so appealing. In fact, the attraction is never ending, for the seasons change, bringing different colours, shapes and sizes of various flowers; new ideas appear, as well as different styles and, as flowers are ephemeral, arrangements need changing frequently, whether they are for the table, the sideboard, the hall or for a party.

I have arranged my book as a series of easy lessons followed by a gallery of pictures that I hope will stimulate you, once you have understood the basic principles, and feel more confident to develop your own tastes and ideas. The last section combines extra information on caring for your flowers, what you need in the way of equipment and accessories, with other useful suggestions.

Sometimes I meet people who want to stop after the first lesson, wanting only to know how to make their flowers look prettier. And, if you remember the principles in the first lesson, by all means stop there. However, if you decide then, or once you have finished the series of step-by-step lessons, that you would like to learn more about this fascinating subject, then you might like to join a flower club, where you will find out more about colour, design, different styles, plants and flowers. As you progress, you may be invited to take part in church festivals, the decorating of stately homes and other historic buildings for charity. This all leads to the study of backgrounds and settings, requiring flowers to complement certain paintings or furniture.

So, whether it is just a bunch of flowers in a vase that you wish to make more attractive or whether you are in search of wanting to know more about the subject, this book, simply written, will help you make a start. Why not begin today?

Julia Clements
Chelsea 1995

Stems of Lilium longiflorum *and gypsophila, with chunks of glass hiding a pin-holder in the base of a shallow dish.*

PART ONE

Beginning

If you have never made an arrangement before, take heart, for it is as easy as ABC. It's all a matter of cutting the stems to different lengths and using various shapes following four basic principles that we will use throughout this step-by-step section:

1 Make your outline first, using thin, fine, long material i.e., decide the width and height of your arrangement.

2 Fill in with shorter flowers.

3 Add shorter but more important flowers low in the centre. This centre is the heart of the design from which all other flowers should appear to emerge, including tall stems (for height) and trailing (for width).

4 Cut your flowers to different lengths and insert some well in, close to the floral foam or wire, i.e., 'recessed', and some coming out, i.e., protruding, to give a three-dimensional effect.

This is all that you will need to know in the beginning.

First Steps

using a pin-holder

In my first lesson, I use a bunch of irises, cut to different lengths.

Step 1 Place a pin-holder (see page 80) in the base of a shallow dish, like the one in the picture, although you could use a soup plate, a large ash tray or any dish deep enough to cover the pin-holder with water.

Step 2 Insert the first tall iris (it can be one and a half times the width of the container), then cut the rest of the irises so that each one comes below the other, the lowest one tilting forward.

Step 3 If the pin-holder shows, add a little piece of wood (picked up in the countryside) or some stones or shells to cover it. Now add water. Easy, isn't it?

Your final arrangement can be made more interesting if you insert a twig and a few snippets from your houseplants to trail over the wood.

Step 1

Step 2

Step 3

Daffodils, Symbols of Spring

using wire netting

I always associate daffodils with March and April, but today these cheerful blooms can be bought in the market and shops as early as December, which I think is a pity. They are probably the most popular spring flowers but many people find their bare stems difficult to arrange unless other material is placed with them, and this is where the evergreen shrubs and twigs, from the garden or countryside, come into their own. (If you use branches or twigs in the summer, do tie them up in a bunch to dry, ready for arrangements at any time of the year.)

Daffodils exude a sticky substance when cut which blocks the stem for water intake so, to help them live longer, squeeze the cut stem ends under a warm running tap to remove this slime. Cut off the white portion of the stem ends, as they drink only from the green part.

Step 2 Add daffodils standing upright in the centre and, as their stems are bare, add some short sprigs of greenery around them.

Step 1 Crumpled wire netting (see page 79) is useful for holding fleshy stems in place. Allow the wire netting to reach an inch or two above the rim of the container and strap it down with sticky tape. Make a triangular outline with stems of golden lonicera and other twigs, making sure the lower ones point forward and backward to avoid a flat effect.

Step 3 Add freesias at the sides and front, finally inserting stems of any shrubs available, such as tassels of Garrya elliptica, Aucuba japonica *(spotted laurel) or pieris. Add water.*

The finished arrangement, to which anemones have been added, is an all-round design with flowers flowing backward and forward over the rim.

A Display of Pink Flowers
using a candle

Flowers can often appear more attractive if lifted high off the table. Here I used a silver cakestand on to which I placed a dish containing a block of water-soaked floral foam (see page 79), which was strapped to the dish with sticky tape. (There is more information on using candles on page 82.)

Step 2 Make the outline of your arrangement by inserting a shorter stem each side of the candle, then a longer one lower down on each side for width, with another one below the candle pointing forward and one pointing backward. I used schizanthus but any blossom or pointed stem would do equally well.

Step 1 Insert a candle in a candle holder into the foam. If using a large candle, make a cradle of toothpicks to hold it firm.

Step 3 Fill in with shorter and more dominant flowers, aiming all stems towards the centre and making sure some of the lower ones point forward. Add water daily.

*A few leaves around the centre unite all the stems in
the finished display – a simple effect easily created.*

A Growing Arrangement

a dish garden

In wintertime or early spring a growing garden is a satisfying arrangement to create. It lasts for weeks and all you need is a few plants, some gravel and soil from the garden centre and a dish. These designs can be effective wherever they are placed and they are an endless source of delight when used in the centre of a table. You can grow your own bulbs to the point of just bursting into flower, or buy them from your favourite florist or garden centre.

Step 2 The finished effect is shown above. The hyacinth and daffodil bulbs were inserted in the centre. In the front and back were inserted small primula plants and ferns. Any small plants can be placed low in the centre and, if there are any spaces, just cover the soil with moss or small pieces of wood. Water when needed but do not let the soil dry out. Watching this garden grow is a delight to all who see it.

Houseplants make a wonderful display when arranged in a dish. Other features, such as this ornament opposite, can be added and the bare soil covered with stones.

Step 1 First, place a layer of gravel in the base of your dish or container for drainage and then add a layer of potting compost. Insert small plants, such as ivy, to trail over the edges and then make holes in the compost ready to insert the bulbs.

Another example of this type of garden made with small houseplants in a brandy glass.

A Spring Show

in contrasting colours

High winds and storms are not welcome by many during the winter but flower arrangers are often delighted by the heaven-sent wealth of broken branches, twigs and roots of upturned trees that festoon the countryside, fields and woods. Here, for free, is the basis of many flower decorations, requiring only an artistic eye to discern which piece to bring back home. Later, you can remove bits you do not want for your arrangement or even add to your piece with the aid of wood glue or headless nails (see pages 86–88).

Step 2 Insert tall stems of bright yellow forsythia, having split the stem ends and given them a long drink beforehand (see page 78).

Step 1 Two-thirds fill a tall vase with sand or pebbles to create a higher platform on which to place a block of floral foam, crumpled wire netting or a pin-holder. Bring the floral foam to above the rim of the container and place the wood across it to give width to your design. If your wood is not exactly like mine, try inserting various twigs into the foam on each side.

Step 3 Add short stems of purple iris in a block of contrasting colour just over the rim pointing forward and also at the back. For the final arrangement (opposite), fill in with any available greenery.

The height of the bright yellow forsythia in a tall vase is balanced by the wood, with purple irises forming a strong contrast in the finished design.

16

Blossom Time

using a cakestand

Blossom! What magic the very word conjures up in our minds during April and May.

Yet if you have a garden and plan your planting carefully, you can have an ornamental shrub or tree giving you blossom throughout the winter.

The blossoming small tree *Prunus subhirtella* 'Autumnalis', which I picked in March, had been in bloom since last October. What a delight this tree is! Even if only a few sprays or twiglets are picked when they are in bud, and brought into the house now and again, you will never fail to bless the day you planted the tree. In the step-by-step pictures you can see how I used the flowering prunus with tulips and hyacinths in an inverted, crescent-style arrangement.

Another flowering tree that delights me for decoration is the *Amelanchier canadensis*, often referred to as snowy mespilus. The branches have twisty ends which, when picked, do not detract from the appearance of the tree which is a mass of blossom in April. Its little starlike flowers are useful for decoration.

Step 2 Insert the stems of blossom to provide width, making sure they flow forwards and downwards.

Step 1 Tie down a block of floral foam with tape to a glass dish of water on top of a cakestand. Make three holes with a dibber and insert the hyacinths. Do remember to squeeze the cut stem ends of hyacinths under a warm running tap to get rid of the slimy substance they exude.

Step 3 Insert the pale and deep pink tulips at the sides and in the centre, some flowing forwards others backwards, and add a few leaves around the centre.

A spare sprig of blossom was added at the back to complete this delicate springtime arrangement.

Tulips in May

four different arrangements

Tulips can be bought in British shops as early as January each year although they would not appear naturally in our gardens until May time. I have often planted special varieties in November only to find that when they appear in May, I cannot bear to cut them, so I resort to buying them, although I cannot always find the colour or variety I would like.

Step 1 Cut off the white portion from the stem ends and stand the tulips in deep water for an hour before arranging. Then place a well-holder (see page 80) in the base of a plant tray or shallow dish.

The same piece of wood is placed across the top of a tall vase to provide the perfect foil for six yellow tulips.

Step 2 Place a twisted piece of wood across the holder and, after cutting the stems still shorter, insert the tulips close together, some at the back of the wood and others in front. (Tulips last much longer when clustered together.)

For a different, unusual approach, use a black bowl with a narrow opening, inserting the flowers close together. For extra effect, add leaves and a piece of red-wired sisal cord, bent to any shape of your choice.

*Here, a dustbin lid was turned upside down to provide
an excellent black base and a striking contrast to some
red tulips, held in a well-holder.*

A Splash of Yellow

in a tall vase

If you are someone who stands a bunch of flowers upright in a vase of water with all the heads at the same level, there is nothing wrong with this, for you are giving them a drink, but it has done nothing for you. You have not expressed yourself and flower arranging is a self-expressive art. So why not try something different? You will certainly feel a great sense of achievement.

Step 2 Although it is not essential, place a twisty dry vine across the opening, pinning it down with a hairpin if you feel it might move, then add some short stems of forsythia in between (see page 80).

For the final display in the tall vase, shown opposite, double yellow tulips have been inserted in a slanting style, with attractive yellow-green evergreen Elaeagnus pungens *'Maculata' in-between, although any short greenery would do.*

Step 1 When using a tall vase, flowers are apt to drop to the bottom leaving the heads just above the rim. So fill the vase two-thirds full with sand or stones to give a higher platform on which to stand a pin-holder in a dish of water, or a well-holder.

As an alternative, use the same material in a low bowl filled with crumpled wire netting or wet floral foam and stand the bowl on a base to give it more importance.

Summer Flowers

an easy approach

Here is a style that anyone could create. All you need is a shallow dish or tray and some floral foam. I used a triangular-shaped plastic dish bought from the garden centre, although any shallow tray would do.

Step 1 Cut slices of well soaked floral foam to fill the dish, allowing it to reach just above the rim. (An ordinary kitchen knife will cut foam effectively.)

Step 3 Add a tall spray of greenery and more short flowers low down to cover the floral foam. To complete the design, insert short sprigs of greenery from your houseplants to fill in the back and front, as in the picture opposite.

Step 2 Establish the height by inserting two stems of larkspur, three fine candles (not to be lit) and a few shorter pinks. These should be spaced forwards and backwards at different levels.

In this simple alternative, you can use three dried strelitzia leaves and five roses.

A decoration like this can last for several weeks if you replace fading flowers with fresh stems, leaving the greenery intact.

A Traditional Summer Display

in a triangular form

Even if you have no garden, many summer flowers are obtainable in markets and shops, enabling you to make a colourful summer display. Do buy your flowers the day before you need them, or even a few hours beforehand. This will give you time to re-cut the stems and stand the flowers in deep water for a long drink.

Although you will develop a style of your own the more you handle flowers, the more you will find that most traditional arrangements are arranged in a triangular shape in either a tall vase or a low bowl.

Step 2 Insert some larger flowers in the centre. I used rambler roses, although any rounder, bigger or more important flowers would do equally well.

Step 1 After placing a block of water-soaked floral foam in the vase and strapping it down with sticky tape, establish the height and width of your arrangement by inserting thin stems of delphiniums.

Step 3 From the sides insert more pink flowers and some lime-green Alchemilla mollis. *Then add a few lilies around the centre and any spare shorter-stemmed delphiniums in-between the central roses with one or two stems low down over the rim, as in the picture opposite.*

The finished arrangement, placed here on a side table, is a classic of its kind and is not difficult to achieve.

Summer Entertaining

on a round table

You may feel that an all-round design for the centre of a table is beyond you, yet it need not be difficult if you start with the height and the width first. Your outline can be made with flowers or leaves, as long as the leaves are thin or fine (larger ones are better used lower down). Pick or buy your flowers in the colour scheme of your choice the day before you need to arrange them if possible. Re-cut the stems and stand in deep water. I used blue larkspur, deep pink roses, 'Doris' pinks and lime-green *Alchemilla mollis* for this arrangement.

Step 3 Add dainty pinks over the outline and flowing low down over the rim back and front.

Touches of lime-green Alchemilla mollis *and white Michaelmas daisies pointing forwards and backwards complete the all-round arrangement opposite, which is standing on a green base.*

Step 1 Fill a low bowl with floral foam or wire netting and strap it down with sticky tape. Insert five stems of larkspur in the height and width you require. If using an oblong table, make the width longer.

Step 2 Cut the roses shorter so that they do not cover the outline and insert some pointing forward, with similar ones at the back.

Alternatively, an oval-shaped display of summer flowers could be used on a side table.

Late Summer Hydrangeas

with wood

Hydrangeas are attractive when used, fresh or dry, and you can add them to other flowers in a big or in a small arrangement. Here I used them with a piece of wood.

If you wish to dry hydrangeas, do not pick them before late September when the small white speck in the middle has died and the bracts are almost dry, with the thickness of tissue-paper. Remove the leaves before arranging them; do not add water but leave the flowers to dry in situ (see pages 89–91).

Step 3 Split the stem ends of the hydrangeas for easier insertion on the well-holder, adding the tallest stems to the design first.

More hydrangeas have been added to complete the final arrangement opposite, one flower being slotted through the wood to soften its bareness.

Step 1 Place a piece of wood on a base or a tray and stand a well-holder behind it. These well-holders come in various shapes; a curved one is excellent for placing behind wood or ornaments.

Step 2 Insert a few stems of foliage on the well-holder for height, although this is not essential.

For an alternative display, fill a bowl with wet floral foam and stand the bowl on a tray. Insert stems of hydrangeas cut to different lengths. I added a bunch of grapes for extra effect but this is optional.

Flowers and Fruit

in a shallow basket

Basketry of all kinds, shapes and sizes associate well with flowers. Round shapes, filled with fruits and vegetables are popular for kitchen arrangements, while filled with dried flowers and placed on a low table they are ideal for looking down upon.

A basket with a handle filled with roses or summer flowers makes a perfect gift to a friend or someone in hospital. But, remember, baskets are not watertight. So use a tin liner or a plastic container inside the basket and, as an additional safeguard, line the basket with heavy polythene. This handled basket, filled with apples and daisies, is pleasant to look at and simple to create.

Step 2 Insert the daisies (marguerites), following the same line and prepare the apples by inserting sticks. I use kebab sticks, which can be obtained in cookery or food shops, but split garden canes will do equally well (see page 81).

Apples have been inserted in-between the daisies opposite, and a few more leaves added to finish this easy-to-make decoration.

Step 1 Place a plastic dish filled with wet floral foam in the base of a basket and insert some fine leaves in a diagonal line, with some stems slanting upwards above the handle, others flowing downwards. I prefer floral foam to wire netting in a basket as there is less possibility of water leaking.

An alternative autumn display, using dahlias, wild dock and fruit.

All-Season Arrangements
in a round basket

Here are four more ways of displaying fruit and flowers in a basket. Don't forget to line all baskets with thick polythene before you begin.

Step 1 Fill a round basket with lemons to above the rim and place small bunches of violets into small medicine tubes of water, inserting these in-between the fruit.

Fill a basket with dry floral foam. Bind small bunches of dried flowers with wire for easier insertion into the foam, as single stems are brittle and may easily break (see page 91). Then insert the bunches in the shape of a mound.

Step 2 Small snippets of greenery complete this attractive basket arrangement.

Fruit and holly fill this basket, which is suitable for a side table at Christmas or for a present.

This handled basket holds several bunches of spring flowers, which were first tied together and inserted into small jars of water.

A Display with a Difference
using a wine rack

When no leaves are available, try a contrasting coloured container or an unusual item from the kitchen as a foil for your flowers. I used a wine rack, which I painted black, and bought one bunch of September Michaelmas daisies (five stems) and one bunch of pink chrysanthemums (five stems) to make this unusual display.

Step 3 Then insert some stems higher and others lower, flowing forward.

Step 1 Fill a plant-pot tray with slices of wet floral foam or, alternatively, use two well-holders filled with water. Then place the wine rack over them.

Step 2 Insert stems of white Michaelmas daisies through the rack into the floral foam in the tray.

This alternative approach uses an upright wine rack, Christmas holly and red carnations on a red base.

*Pink chrysanthemums finish this eye-catching
arrangement with Michaelmas daisies, but roses or
dahlias would look just as effective.*

Autumn Arrangements

using pieces of wood

Wood is a natural adjunct to flowers in decoration. One piece can add another dimension to just a few flowers, giving them added texture and colour. All kinds of shapes can be discovered in the countryside which can be polished, painted, made bigger or smaller, or simply left as found (see pages 86–88). Any one piece will offer different possibilities each time you use it, as the pictures here suggest.

This small branch was first laid flat on a black base. The leaves and colourful asters were inserted into a well-holder at the back, with some of the flowers pointing forwards over the wood to avoid a flat effect.

This piece of wood would not stand square, so I drilled a hole and inserted a dowel stick with glue, which helped it stand in the position I desired (see page 87). I then placed a well-holder behind the wood, inserted the tall golden privet leaves, followed by short, pink chrysanthemums. Finally, I added some large bergenia leaves to the left to balance the daintiness of the chrysanthemums.

Standing upright on a sawn-off base, the same piece of wood now blends with white Michaelmas daisies in a well-holder.

Hydrangeas are used here instead of privet and chrysanthemums. Some of the flowers lean forward, covering the wood, to create a unified effect.

Autumn Favourites

two ways with chrysanthemums

The chrysanthemum is one flower that is always available, all the year round, yet I try to avoid using it until late autumn and winter. But I do admit it is useful for those living in town and it has the additional advantage of lasting a long time.

The flowers come in many colours and varieties and with a few stems you can try out various designs. Here I show two quite different approaches but the more you become interested in the subject, the more easily you will discover styles of your own.

Step 2 Cover this outline with shorter material, such as Michaelmas daisies, adding a stem to each side of the central stem. Then cut short some pink chrysanthemums, ready to finish the arrangement as shown below.

Step 1 Fill a bowl with floral foam, allowing it to reach an inch or more above the rim, then make a triangular shape with any tall fine stems.

Short stems of pink spray chrysanthemums, some pointing forward over the rim and some low down at the back, complete this autumn picture.

Alternatively, pink chrysanthemums can be clustered at the top of a tall container with a thick stem of geranium.

Autumn Harmony

in pink and white

The *Nerine bowdenii* makes a happy change from chrysanthemums for autumn and winter flower arrangements, its clear sugar-pink colouring blending well with almost everything.

There are, of course, other colours in this family, the flowers having been hybridized from the wild ones which grow so profusely in South Africa. Today they can be bought on the market as cut flowers. I use the bright pink variety *ancilla* with Michaelmas daisies.

Step 2 Add the nerines, one to give height and the lower one protruding forward.

Step 1 Fill a shallow dish with water-soaked floral foam, or crumpled wire netting, then make a triangular outline with the stems of Michaelmas daisies, making sure the low front stem points forward over the rim.

Step 3 Then add stems of Euphorbia marginata *in-between the nerines to break up the colour, placing some leaning back and others low and forward. This flower is useful when leaves are unobtainable but do be careful when picking it as the milky substance it exudes may cause an irritation to the skin.*

The finished arrangement of carmine-pink nerines and
white Michaelmas daisies offers a delicate alternative
to some of autumn's stronger colours.

Harvest Gold

with vegetables and fruit

During autumn and winter, gardens are abundant with fruit and vegetables, so it makes sense to combine some of this richness with your flowers.

The hedgerows are full of goodies – there are berries galore, wild rosehips, hawthorn berries, seedheads, grasses, nuts and cones, all of which combine well with a few chrysanthemums or any other winter flowers of your choice.

Yellow and orange groups go well with chestnuts, cobnuts, autumn-coloured foliage and dry branches.

In this autumn arrangement, I used two beige covered bases, resting on top of each other with a bowl in-between.

Step 2 Back the outline with evergreen variegated Euonymus. Then add some stems of chrysanthemums, following the outline.

Step 1 Fill a dish with water-soaked floral foam and strap it down with tape. Next, place the first stem to the right of centre, to make an off-centre outline with Solidago (golden rod).

Step 3 If you wish to add grapes, now is the time to put them in, fixing them to the floral foam with a strong hairpin. You can thread some more stems through the grapes, so that the grapes are tucked inside. Fresh grapes are preferable, but plastic ones look equally good in decoration.

A few pyracantha berries have been added to the centre of the finished piece, and fruit, corn cobs, tomatoes and mushrooms placed on the lower base.

As an alternative, for a blue room, why not try an arrangement of pink dahlias, dark red apples and purple grapes?

A Modern Approach

using cane

Styles come and go and the more you become interested in flowers, the more styles you will want to attempt.

Here I used six bamboo garden canes as the outline of this modern style. I painted the canes a lime green, although you could paint them differently according to your colour scheme, or you could leave them plain. Leave three of the canes for height about 22–24in. (55–60cm) tall and cut the other three in halves so that one half is 2in. (5cm)

longer than the other. Use any flowers of your choice but remember they should be clustered together, whether they be roses, chrysanthemums, azaleas or other flowers in season. Use only tall, upright flowers in a deep vase, as smaller flowers are apt to fall to the bottom. So try using a bowl or a plastic plant tray on top of the vase and fill it with a block of floral foam, strapping the whole block down with tape. In this case I filled the container with a block of wet floral foam.

Step 1 Insert the three long canes in the centre, followed by three shorter canes pointing downwards, with the other three pointing upwards. This forms the outline of the design. If you cut the canes on a slant they will be easier to work with.

Step 2 Insert the carnations on a slant, making sure you place some at the back behind the tall canes. Lime-green Alchemilla mollis, a favourite with flower arrangers, gives the final design a framework, and two hosta leaves provide a change of form.

Windowsill Flowers

in the parallel style

I find this parallel style very useful for a long dining table, the ledge of a church window or for any shelf or windowsill. It is easy to make, for you do not have to study rhythm or balance. The finished effect should appear like a growing herbaceous garden border. You could copy it in autumn or winter, using bare branches for height or candles with preserved leaves, and cones low down, or using holly and red glass baubles. There are all kinds of variations.

Step 1 Cut a block of wet floral foam in half length-wise, strapping it down to a plant-pot tray with sticky tape. Next, insert a few pink larkspur at the left with a similar group of blue, shorter larkspur to the right. Add a few pieces of greenery to start covering the rim of the tray.

Step 2 Insert a few shorter flowers upright in the centre and below both sets of the tall ones. My roses opened rather large in the heat but any flowers would do equally well.

Step 3 Next, add a few short flowers, such as godetia or cornflowers, low near the rim and tilting forward. Add some greenery to finish, as shown opposite above. Whatever extra flowers you put in the front of the arrangement, you should also carry through to the back.

In the finished design, more short flowers and pieces of greenery have been added to cover the foam and the rim of the tray.

This variation in a round dish includes snowdrops (in small bottles of water), primulas and winter twigs (in wet foam).

A Pyramid

using a cone

This conical shape is a modern version of a style of decoration that was popular in sixteenth-century Europe.

Today it is useful for tight spaces, such as alcoves, and a number of pyramids, when completed, can look very effective placed at intervals down a long banqueting table.

The style can be made with dried flowers, or with short sprigs of holly at Christmas time. I have also made it with cones of fruit, such as satsumas, interspersed with holly.

However, here I have used a bunch of only one type of flower (choose your own favourite), which can easily be put together to create an attractive style for a small space.

Step 2 Insert a short stem at the top for height and place short flowers firstly round the rim at the bottom, then filling the gaps in-between in the second ring.

Step 1 Fill a container to the rim with wet floral foam and insert a stick in the centre. Then, after soaking another block of foam in water, cut it to the shape of a cone, not too thin at the top, and insert this block on to the stick which will keep it firm.

Step 3 Continue upwards by adding shorter flowers closer to the foam to form the cone-like shape. To water the final display (opposite), use a spray or trickle a little down from the top.

Sprigs of greenery or tips of houseplants have been slipped into the cone between the flowers and around the rim for the final effect.

One for Every Season

four ways with one container

A container is anything that will hold water. It can be made of china, pottery, wood, glass, basketry or metal, and be any household item, such as a teapot, vegetable dish, brass kettle or jug (see page 79). As your interest in flower arranging grows, so will your collection of containers. Although some people say that they like a certain style, but do not have the right container, I feel that almost any style can be adapted to almost any container. Only you can decide if you like the effect. Soon you will discover that wood does not go well with fine china or glass and that delicate flowers are not compatible with heavy pottery. As a student of the art of flower arranging, you will learn later about textures. Here I show you four different ways of using the same container.

In late summer, insert stems of Leycesteria formosa *into a pin-holder in the base of the container. Finish with five single chrysanthemums and some crab apples.*

For a winter arrangement, fill the container with floral foam to reach above the rim, or use wire netting, and insert all kinds of twigs, catkins and greenery.

In autumn, insert some bleached ivy twigs onto a pin-holder, then add two beautiful belladonna lilies, surrounding these with large, leathery-looking bergenia leaves.

*In spring, hold a heavy piece of wood firm to the rim of
the container with soft modelling material. Insert the
blossom and five pink tulips on one side with some
short grape hyacinths on the other.*

A Church Arrangement

on a larger scale

Many of you will want to stop these lessons once you have grasped the way to make flowers look prettier for the home. But some of you will want to continue and soon you may be asked to help with flowers for church or for a family wedding. Here you will need more flowers, i.e., tall for the outline, bigger ones for the central interest and medium-sized ones for filling in and the sides. You will also need a bigger container, or bowl, filled with water-soaked floral foam placed well above the rim.

Step 1 Strap the foam down to the container and, if using tall heavy flowers, cover the foam with a piece of crumpled wire netting to give extra support. Then insert the stems of greenery. Have water in the bowl at the outset.

Step 2 Insert tall larkspur or delphiniums for height, adding carnations low for the sides. Shorter larkspur should lean backwards.

Step 3 Add some lilies or larger dahlias in the centre, the lower ones pointing forward over the rim.

A quick, easy arrangement for church can be achieved by surrounding a tall candlestick with two bunches of gypsophila held firm in a ring of floral foam.

*Shorter flowers aimed at the centre, more leaves to give
depth and ivy to unite the bowl and pedestal were
added to complete this church arrangement in white.*

Christmas Colour

using candles

Long before electricity lightened our hours of darkness, candles provided the only illumination for our streets. The candles supplied by the tallow chandlers were made from animal fat and were coarser than those made of the sweeter-smelling beeswax used mainly in churches and the homes of the wealthy.

Today, they are made in all shapes, sizes and colours to suit every known decorative occasion. Variously coloured candles can add to your colour scheme whether contrasting or harmonious, whether lighted or left unlit as part of the plan.

Here I show one of the easiest ways of making a Christmas table centrepiece with candles.

Step 2 Add short sprigs of holly, or other greenery.

Step 1 Cut a block of wet floral foam lengthwise and place it in a tray, strapping it down with tape. Insert four candles of different heights.

In the finished Christmas centrepiece, a few coloured glass baubles complete the effect. False red berries or small bows of red ribbon are suitable alternatives.

Another idea for Christmas – a hanging decoration in which three lots of floral foam were fixed to a broad strip of red felt and filled with holly and baubles.

PART TWO

Inspiration

Flower arranging is a creative subject and, although in the beginning you may only want to make your flowers look more attractive, as you continue, the more you will want to invent something for yourself. The finished arrangements that follow are designed to inspire you to develop your own talents.

Be Yourself

Arranging flowers is not unlike cooking. You may know how to cook a certain dish from following the recipe but you may often feel like adding a different herb or a little more salt – in this way you make the dish your own. In the same way, an artist has to have a landscape or model from which to get started; he or she can then add their own ideas to make it their own portrait or landscape and not just a photograph. And so it is with flowers.

You may, for example, after looking at a picture in the step-by-step section of the book, want to add an extra leaf or to use a different colour to the one given in the lesson. Try different ways of arranging the same flowers, adding little touches of your own. As long as the display is balanced, i.e., not top heavy, you will be surprised at what you can achieve. Try, too, not to use a mass of heavy flowers on top of a delicate container, or small flowers in a large, heavy pottery one. (I cover these suggestions in more detail in my book *Flower Arranging For All Occasions*.)

So, as soon as you have the techniques of getting the flowers into a container and you know how to care for them to help them live longer (see pages 76–78), the whole new world of flower arranging will be open to you. You will never again walk down the garden, in the countryside, in the woods, or even along the seashore, without being conscious of some object, piece of wood, flower or leaf that will help you make an arrangement of your own.

To achieve this style, you only need two chrysanthemum stems, rosehip berries and a twisted piece of root wood.

A summer display suitable for a formal setting. Dainty pinks and other fine stems were inserted into water-soaked floral foam after the tall blue delphiniums.

Ornamental Elegance

Simple but sophisticated, both these displays feature ornaments. To the right, roses cluster around the base of the ornament, which is supported by toothpicks in wet floral foam. Alchemilla mollis *adds a dainty finishing touch. Below, the ornament is part of an imaginative scene using a branch of* Cornus mas.

Early Blossom

A grand display suitable for a living-room side table, using sprays of Amelanchier (snowy mespilus), filled in with shorter daffodils, lilies and a few contrasting anemones inserted into wire netting.

Purple and Gold

Two imaginative displays of spring irises with contrasting yellow Cornus mas *(right) and forsythia (below). Both are finished with a few* Arum italicum *leaves, an invaluable winter stand-by for the flower arranger.*

Tranquillity

Eye-catching yet restful – two lovely camellias and a little tree ivy, with a dry, twisty branch held firm across the top of the container.

Modern Harmony

Using fewer flowers than in a traditional arrangement, two clivias (right) form a stylish contrast with modern pottery and wood, while irises, oranges and Alchemilla mollis *look dramatic with a piece of ivy root painted black (below).*

Simplicity

Often just a rose or a peony with a branch is all that is necessary to make an effective decoration. Here I combined a Lilium longiflorum *with wood and tree ivy (right) and one stem of amaryllis with wood and a couple of sprigs of pine (below).*

A Golden Christmas

Gold baubles and orange satsumas create a glowing centrepiece (right), while winter foliage and fruit make an attractive arrangement for a buffet table (below).

Showpiece

*Finally, you may well aspire to enter a show one day.
Here are two interpretations of class titles in recent
National Association of Flower Arrangement Societies
(NAFAS) shows: (below) 'Where Dragons Dwell' by
Susan Phillips at Buxton and (right) 'Altered Images'
by Judith Butterworth at Manchester*

PART THREE

Finishing Touches

Now you have learnt how easy it is to arrange flowers attractively and have seen what can be achieved once you let your own imagination run free, you will probably find it useful to learn more about looking after flowers, what equipment and accessories you will need, how to use colour, make the most of wood, or dry flowers for the winter months. Finally, I suggest some tips on how to take advantage of what each season has to offer to flower arrangers.

Caring for Your Flowers

Nothing is more disappointing than to find that some of the flowers in your arrangement have wilted within a day, so spoiling the entire design that you have so thoughtfully created.

In the beginning, you need only to know that you should re-cut the stems of *all* flowers after picking or buying and then stand them in deep, tepid water for several hours before arranging them. This will fully charge the stems with water, so helping them to live longer.

As you progress, learning more about different varieties of flowers and shrubs and leaves, you may want to know more about what is termed 'conditioning your plant material'. In case you are faced with the problem of limp leaves, or drooping roses, or the soft heads of hydrangeas, the following advice might be helpful:

🌿 **Always pick flowers** before they are fully mature.

🌿 **Flowers should be picked at night or early in the morning**, whenever possible, when loss of water is at its lowest. During the day, flowers lose water through evaporation (this is called transpiration).

🌿 **Tulips** will always turn to face the light. Pierce the stems just under the heads with a pin and then wrap them in wet newspaper so that the stem and flower are well supported. Plunge the newspaper-wrapped flowers into deep water and leave overnight or for several hours.

🌿 *Begonia rex* and other rather soft-leaved houseplants, if cut and used in decorations, should first be submerged for a few hours in water to which a teaspoon (5ml) of sugar has been added.

🌿 **Blossoming sprays** can be forced into early flowering if they are first submerged in warm water to swell the buds and then, after slitting the stem ends, placed in warm water in a warm room. This will only work if the blossom is picked when the buds are swollen and ready to burst.

🌿 **All flowers** should have their lower leaves stripped off and their stems re-cut under water. This is particularly important for hollow-stemmed plants as it will avoid an airlock forming in the stem that will prevent the flower from taking water. The stems should be cut at an angle which will give a wider exposed area than a straight horizontal cut, allowing the flower to take in the maximum amount of water. The re-cut flowers should be left in deep water for several hours, or overnight, in a dark, airy place before being arranged. This treatment will harden the stems and allow them to become fully loaded with water.

Cutting a stem under water to prevent an airlock.

✺ **Jointed stems**, such as carnations and sweet Williams, should have their stems cut at an angle just above one of the joints.

✺ **Leaves and sprays of greenery** should be submerged in water for a few hours before being arranged, but be careful as leaves that are soaked too long lose their texture. Only experience will tell you how long to soak different varieties of leaves. Soaking does not apply to leaves that have a woolly texture or are heavily covered with hairs. Lamb's tongue (*Stachys lanata*) is one of these varieties and will soak up water like a sponge, resulting in it losing its beautiful grey tones. Woolly textured leaves should have their stems dipped into boiling water for one to two minutes, taking care to protect the leaves from the hot steam by wrapping them in paper. The leaves should then be conditioned in shallow water.

✺ **Camellia, rhododendron, laurel, fatsia** and other large-surfaced, shiny leaves can have their shine prolonged if they are wiped over occasionally with a damp cloth sprinkled with a few drops of oil. There are also commercial products, available from florists and garden centres, that do the same job.

✺ **Always have warm water** in the container or vase you are arranging into as this will prevent the ends of the stems from drying while you work. A tablet of charcoal, available from florists' shops, in the water will help to keep it pure. Check the level of the water every day and top up with tepid water if necessary.

✺ **When placing flowers in deep water to condition them**, make sure the containers are spotlessly clean and are the correct size for the flowers. Do not place short-stemmed flowers in with long-stemmed ones as these may crush the smaller flowers or drink so much water that the shorter stems are left clear of the water.

✺ **Gourds**, which form the basis of many dried arrangements, should be picked when fully ripe and the skins are hard, then placed on a sheet of newspaper in a warm room or cupboard to dry. Try to leave a short stem on the gourds as this makes wiring easier, if needed. They should be checked regularly and any transpiration wiped off with a cloth.

✺ **Delphiniums and lupins** and other similar flowers, will benefit if the hollow stems are filled with water after cutting and then plugged with cotton wool, before being left overnight in deep water.

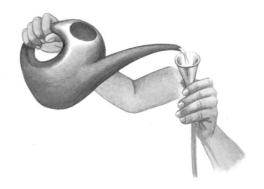

Filling a hollow stem with water, using a small funnel and a watering can.

✺ **A fine spray of water around the arrangement in hot weather** will help to counteract the loss of moisture through transipiration. These sprays can be bought from garden centres and hardware shops.

🌸 **When you pick flowers from your own garden**, take with you a bucket filled with water so that the stems can be placed in water as soon as they are cut.

🌸 **The stem ends of daffodils, narcissi, hyacinths** and similar flowers should be held under warm running water to remove the sticky sap they exude. If this is not done, the sap forms a seal over the end of the stems making it more difficult for the flowers to take in water.

🌸 **Exotic flowers**, such as anthuriums, orchids and strelitzias, although very long lasting, will benefit if the stem ends are re-cut after a week to remove the brown stain that often appears. If this is allowed to remain, it will attract bacteria.

🌸 **Roses** will last longer if the lower leaves and thorns are removed and the stem ends split before they are placed in water. Wilting roses, which have been left out of water for some time or have arrived by post, should be treated in the same way before being placed in near-boiling water to which a teaspoon (5ml) of sugar has been added. There are also several commercial products which, when added to the water instead of sugar, will revive wilting flowers. Most flowers will last longer if sugar is added to the water in the container they are arranged in. (This does not apply to daffodils and narcissi which exude a sticky slime.)

Use 1 teaspoon (5ml) of sugar to 1 pint (600ml) of water.

🌸 **When using floral foam to hold the flowers in place**, make sure it has been well saturated with water. This will take about half an hour. Leave a space at the back of the vase where more water can be added daily.

🌸 **Keep all flower arrangements away from the hot sun or cold draughts**, even if this means you must move them from time to time. It will be worth it.

🌸 **Make sure that you always remove the white portion** at the stem ends of bulbous flowers, such as early tulips and daffodils, as they only drink from the green portion.

🌸 **Hellebores and anemones** will stand up strongly if a pin is drawn down the side of the stem from top to bottom before leaving them to stand in deep tepid or warm water prior to arranging.

🌸 **All woody-stemmed flowers**, such as lilac, viburnum, outdoor chrysanthemums, roses and other flowering trees and shrubs, should have some of their lower leaves removed and the bottom 1½in. (4cm) of their stems split before they are placed in deep water. Using a sharp knife, or scissors, scrape the lower 1½in. (4cm) of the outside covering (the bark) off the stem to expose the inner tissue. Split the exposed stem lengthwise.

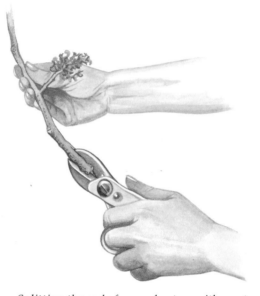

Splitting the end of a woody stem with secateurs.

In conclusion, the best way to perfect the conditioning of flowers is to experiment but, to simplify matters, always remember:

🌸 **All flowers** should have their stems cut under water if possible, and then be left to stand in deep water for several hours before being arranged.

🌸 **All woody-type stems** should be split before standing them in deep water.

🌸 **Most leaves** should be submerged in water for a few hours before use.

🌸 **Warm water** should be used in your container and topped up each day.

If you follow these rules, your flowers should stay fresh and be a source of joy to all who see them.

Equipment and Accessories

You will need very little in the way of equipment to begin with – a few containers, a pin-holder, some wire netting, floral foam and a good pair of kitchen scissors. You can collect other items and accessories, such as candle cups, gradually.

Containers

As you will have seen in the step-by-step lessons, choosing a container is important as it is as much part of your design as the flowers. The drawings on this page show a few basic containers, apart from tall vases and jugs. However, if you keep your eyes open, you will see that wood, pottery, baskets and pieces of scrap metal all offer fascinating possibilities as containers.

A traditional container for formal arrangements.

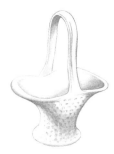

A china basket for small flowers like snowdrops.

A bowl for floral foam, although any bowl will do.

A shallow dish for modern designs.

A bottle, with a funnel to help you use more flowers.

Holders

A well designed display relies on flowers being held in place firmly. The most useful items for this job are wire netting, floral foam and pin-holders.

Floral foam is a plastic substance that absorbs water. It can be found in garden centres, florists' shops and department stores under various brand names. Large pieces can be cut with a knife and should be soaked in water for about thirty minutes before using for your display.

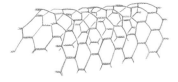

Wire netting, available from hardware shops, is cheaper and more long lasting than foam. Crumple it first, then push it well down into the container, leaving a little exposed above the rim. A 2in. (5cm) mesh is suitable for average use but a finer one is better for smaller flowers.

Pin-holders are available in a variety of shapes and sizes from florists and garden centres. Use them in shallow dishes or for extra support in larger arrangements beneath wire netting.

A well-holder is a pin-holder welded into a heavy metal cup that holds water. It is ideal for use behind ornaments or wood, or in shallow dishes and baskets.

For a display of fruit and flowers, hairpins will hold grapes while larger fruit, such as pineapples, can be inserted into a cradle of sticks, which themselves are inserted into foam.

It is sometimes difficult to insert hard stems or wood into pin-holders. Toothpicks tied to the stems with wire make the job much easier.

The protruding foam in the funnel when placed in a narrow-necked container allows for flowers to be inserted at an angle to provide a balanced display.

A hairpin is handy for holding a single branch horizontally to floral foam. If you don't have a hairpin, use a piece of stub wire.

Cones

Use cones, available from florists and garden centres, to give extra height to short stems. While they do give some support, you will need to fill them with water-soaked floral foam first.

Three cones, secured to bamboo canes, inserted into crumpled wire netting. They should not be visible in the final arrangement.

Tools

On this page I cover any remaining items of equipment that you will find useful when you begin flower arranging. Set aside a box or drawer to keep everything together so you can find it easily.

Floral scissors have a useful serrated edge but kitchen scissors will do just as well.

Secateurs are essential for cutting thick and woody stems and small branches.

Use the thicker stub wire for holding a branch in place and thinner reel wire for binding toothpicks and adding false stems to leaves. Use ordinary sticky tape for holding foam in place and binding stems.

Kebab sticks, toothpicks and bamboo canes are all useful as cradles and supports.

You can use any shape for a base. I cover a cardboard cakestand from a stationer's with different material to suit my flowers.

Candles and candle cups

I am very fond of using candles and candlesticks with flowers to create some calm, peaceful effects, using light and colour harmoniously.

You will need some candle cups, which are shallow metal or plastic bowls on stems, available from florists. Spray them different colours if necessary to suit your arrangements. Candle holders (see page 12) are also useful. A ring of soft modelling material can be moulded around the base of the cup to hold it firmly in the candlestick. The cup is then filled with a small block of water-soaked floral foam.

A candle in a candle holder inserted into floral foam with the additional support of wire netting all within the candle cup can also provide the basis for an arrangement.

USING CANDLES

❧ Before using, keep in the fridge overnight to slow down burning time.

❧ If the ends are too large for the candlestick, dip them in hot water to soften.

❧ As a centrepiece, surround a single large candle with toothpicks in floral foam.

❧ To extinguish and to avoid spilling wax, place your forefinger across your mouth and blow over it.

Playing with Colour

Not everyone who arranges flowers wants to know about colour. If you know what you like, that is fine but you may like some help in complementing your room furnishings with similarly coloured flowers, or in picking up the colouring of your china on the dining table. Later, if you are in competition work at a show you will need to know more for, by interpreting a class title, colour can be an important factor with the judges. For instance, if the title calls for a welcoming arrangement in a dark hall, you will need to know about cheerful, light colours, such as yellow, orange or white. If you used your favourite blue delphiniums, with other deep-coloured flowers and dark leaves, it would be passed over by the judge, for blue is a receding colour and would not show up in a dark hall. Similarly, blue flowers are not the best for most churches for they will fade into oblivion, especially when seen from a distance. Better to use yellow, white, orange or pale pink, although in many Scottish churches, which have white walls, a background of leaves will help project the light colours of the flowers.

Colour is a vast subject and cannot really be covered in this book. However, it would be useful for you to know that yellow is considered to be a cheerful colour, blue and violet subdued, red is exciting, green is tranquil, and reddish-purple is royal. Certain colours are contrasting, such as numbers 1 and 7 or 5 and 10 on the colour chart opposite. Others are harmonious, such as numbers 1 to 4. Advancing warm colours are 9 to 12; receding or cool, 2 to 5.

So, I hope that you enjoy experimenting with colours even if you do finish with a mixed bunch!

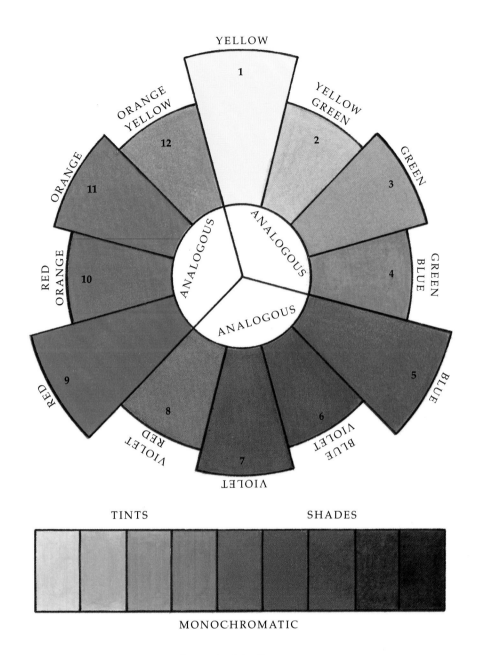

A colour wheel for flower arrangers.

DEFINITIONS OF COLOUR TERMS

Primary colours are red, yellow and blue.

Secondary colours are green, violet and orange.

Tertiary colours are yellow green, green blue, blue violet, violet red, red orange and orange yellow.

Hue – the name of a colour, i.e., a hue of red.

Tint – a lighter version of a colour.

Shade – a darker version of a colour.

Tone – a dulled or greyed version of a colour.

Analogous – tints and shades of colours lying adjacent to each other on the wheel, i.e., 1 to 4 or 9 to 12. To include only one primary colour.

A monochromatic design in blue, i.e., a play on one colour (above) and an autumn arrangement of analogous colours, i.e., those close to each other on the colour wheel (right)

Working with Wood

A few stems of dried white statice tucked in-between two pieces of root wood, one on top of the other.

We used to call it driftwood, in fact many of us still do, but 'driftwood' does not fully describe the great variety of wood that arrangers use today. In addition to the pieces that can be found on the seashore or by the banks of lakes, many interesting items can be found in woods or by the country roadside. Stumps of upturned trees show fascinating shapes; limbs of trees torn off by storms and roots that have been exposed to the elements lie around waiting for a 'seeing eye' to notice their possibilities.

And that is not all: just think of the wonderfully rhythmic swerves that occur naturally in a bare branch of honeysuckle, a vine, ivy or the type of branch that clings to the bark of an old tree. This can be pulled off and laid across the neck of a container to form the width for an imaginative design (see page 66–67). Tendrils of contorted ivy twigs will give height to many compositions in low dishes (see page 52). The wispy ends of roots will create an eerie atmosphere around some delicate flowers, especially if you spray-paint the root-ends with a metallic black paint, obtainable from motor-accessory shops (see page 68).

The possibilities are enormous and, because I look upon weathered wood as Nature's sculptures, I never tire of using it. I can see a different design every time I study a piece of 'found' wood: sometimes I visualize it standing up and then lying down, as on page 38; at other times I think a flower placed protruding from the side would make a dramatic picture; later I feel a small cluster nestling in the crevice could be more effective. I might use a base to give the wood more stability (see page 38); at other times I have mounted wood on a dowel stick to give it the appearance of lightness. The fun of using wood is never ending – its various forms, sizes and shapes are always fascinating and, if you do not like the shape of the piece you have found, you can either saw a piece off or add on another piece.

Some flower arrangers have suggested that wood is best used at shows, where it is termed 'natural plant material', or in country settings, but I have some beautiful, smooth-polished pieces that are perfectly in keeping with period furniture.

Cleaning wood

Of course, before using 'found' wood in the home it should be cleaned. Submerge your discovered pieces in a bath of water to which detergent and disinfectant have been added. This will loosen odd soft pieces and should kill any insects that might be hidden inside the wood. After drying, the wood should be brushed with a stiff or wire brush, and the crevices and grooves should be scraped out with a pointed knife to remove decayed fungus and rotted wood. An old toothbrush or bottle brush is useful for cleaning out difficult parts. Tree ivy can have its bark removed as soon as it is picked, so leaving a white, smooth interior but, if left for a while, it is best to submerge it in strong soda water for several hours. The bark can then be peeled off more easily, ready for it to be bleached or painted.

When your wood is dry and free of dust, you can shape it how you like. With the aid of woodworking glue and headless screws or nails, you can add a portion to give a better line. The surfaces can be sandblasted or polished smooth but, in all cases, rub it over with a colourless wax or furniture polish in order to preserve it.

Removing soft wood with a knife.

Brushing with a wire brush.

Supporting wood

Many flower arrangers have difficulty in finding the correct support for wood. Unfortunately, there is no one single method, for each piece is different. An item can be sawn off at the base to help it stand firm or it can be nailed to another portion of flat wood, the flat support then being placed in a low dish. Alternatively, a tin lid can be nailed to the base of the wood and the edges of the lid then inserted on to a pin-holder. If the pieces are fairly light, they can be inserted directly into floral foam or a pin-holder. However, if the wood is hard or heavy, try wrapping thick hairpins round the base of the branch with clear adhesive tape or wire and glue and then inserting the ends of the pins into the foam or pin-holder.

Nailing a flat piece of wood to some ivy roots.

Dowel sticks can also be inserted into larger pieces of wood to give a supporting leg (see page 38). Drill a hole first, insert the dowel and then fix it with adhesive. Should you want your wood to hang down the face of a tall pottery container, an extra dowel leg can be added, the dowel going inside the container, the branch or twig outside. If the neck of the vase is narrow, I sometimes use strong wire wrapped around the wood, the wire being inserted inside the container, thus allowing the branch to hang downwards outside.

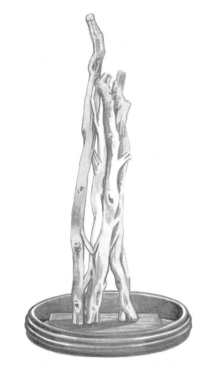

Ivy roots standing upright on a wooden base in a shallow container.

The methods vary with the shape of the wood and the size or shape of the container but, once you start thinking about the decorative use of wood, a whole new world will open up before you.

Colouring wood

Sprayed with metallic grey paint, this piece of wood now stands on a base in a modern container.

If a change of colour is needed, you can use various coloured shoe polishes or wood stain. The attractive 'greyed' pieces of wood bleached by sun and water, often found at the seaside or by the edges of lakes, I leave as found but, with other pieces, I have successfully altered the surfaces, in order to better associate with some flowers, by giving them a thin solution of paint, then wiping down with a cloth before allowing them to dry (this leaves particles of paint in the crevices). Pastel chalks rubbed over the wood will give a similar effect. Another very good idea to give colour, which does not conceal the texture of the wood, is to make up a mixture of 1 cup (225ml) of clear ammonia , 2 tablespoons (30ml) of copper powder (from hardware or art shops) and 2 or 3 tablespoons (30–45ml) of white glue. Paint this on to the wood and, as it dries, the mixture will oxidize to provide a lovely blue-green patina. I used half this quantity for one tall piece of wood, so the amount will depend upon the size of the surface you wish to cover.

Wood can also be carved, then varnished, before being mounted on a base.

Learning to Dry Flowers

In 1947 I was first introduced to the drying of flowers in three dimensions when I was asked by the New York Botanical Gardens to exhibit an orchid which they claimed had come from the top of Princess Elizabeth's wedding cake before it had been dehydrated in powdered borax. What follows is a fascinating story which I related in my book *My Life with Flowers*. Of course, the Victorians used certain dried flowers such as ferns, grasses and the orange-coloured Chinese lanterns, but this drying in three dimensions seemed to be new.

Dried flowers were never meant to take the place of fresh flowers or foliage but they are certainly timesavers, for they can be made up in advance and brought out only when needed. In most homes there is nearly always one place where a permanent arrangement of dried material can stand when flowers are scarce or expensive. These arrangements need not be dull. Indeed, some of the

A vase of contrasting colour will often bring a few dried flowers to life. Here, white statice and silvery honesty pods are arranged with pink everlasting acrocliniums in a turquoise-blue glass vase.

most lovely designs are composed of dried summer flowers, the colours of which can be preserved by hanging them upside down in a dark, dry cupboard.

There are several different methods of preserving material, and after a little experimenting you will quickly become accustomed to using the one that suits your purpose.

The upside-down method

This method of drying is used for flowers such as delphiniums, larkspur, astilbes, golden rod, celosia, helichrysum, achillea and many others. They should be picked just before maturity and hung upside down in small bunches in a dark, dry cupboard or attic, preferably where air circulates. The dry atmosphere will absorb any moisture quickly and the darkness will prevent the fading of the colours. Flowers can be left hanging until required.

Borax method

The burying-in-borax method, (powdered alum can be added), is mostly used for more open flowers such as Canterbury bells, pansies, zinnias, marguerites, daffodils and scabious, for in this manner the three-dimensional form of the flowers can be preserved as well as the colour.

You will require a deep box, the bottom of which should be covered with powdered borax. Strip all leaves from the flowers and shorten the stems, then stand them on the borax and continue to put more powder around, under and over the flowers until they are completely covered. Smooth out the petals as you cover them, so as to retain the original shape and leave in this powder for about three weeks. The powder should then be poured off, or removed with a soft brush very carefully, as the petals will now be rather brittle. Silver sand can also be used for drying flowers but make sure the sand and flowers are dry, otherwise mildew or brown spots will form.

Both these methods have now been superseded by the use of powdered silica gel, which is more expensive but can be used again and dries flowers in about three days.

Binding a dried flower stem with tape for support.

Pouring powdered silica gel over open-faced flowers to dry them in three dimensions.

Glycerine and water method

Most foliage is preserved by this method and branches of leaves placed in this solution will keep indefinitely.

Wash the leaves to remove dust and split the ends of the stems or branches to allow the solution to be more readily absorbed. Place the material in a jar containing one part glycerine and two parts hot water, which should reach about 4in. (10cm) up the stem.

Leave for two or three weeks in a place where air circulates, otherwise the leaves may dry out before the solution reaches the tips. Beech, laurel, magnolia, rhododendron, camellia and pittosporum can all be preserved in this way, although the leaves will turn brown. Mottled effects can be obtained if some leaves are removed at the halfway stage.

Smaller leaves, such as ivy and lily of the valley, preserve much better if the whole leaf is submerged.

Pressing method

Ferns and other flat-surfaced leaves are preserved by the pressing-between-newspaper method. Although they remain flat, some very interesting lines and shapes can be retained. A warm iron pressed over the newspaper will hasten the drying.

Hosta and vine leaves can be folded double and placed between sheets of newspaper, while iris, gladioli, ivy, raspberry leaves and all ferns can be dried in the same way, although it must be remembered the leaves will be brittle and not pliable as with the glycerine method. Plenty of newspaper should be used to absorb the moisture from the leaves and weighty objects, such as books, should be placed on top of the pile to ensure even pressure.

Other ideas

The subject of drying material is a vast but very absorbing one and, if you are keen to pursue it, I do advise you to keep your eyes open for all kinds of seedheads, such as poppy and love-in-the-mist, and material which will make interesting lines, such as dock and dry branches. Do not forget the value of grains and grasses, while cones, pods, nuts, fruits, globe artichokes and gourds are excellent for focal interest.

Pussy willow and bulrushes dry well if kept out of water, otherwise they go to seed. Interesting shapes can be obtained with broom if you wrap it in newspaper, bend it to the desired shape and then leave it to dry in this position.

Another item that attracts the keen flower arranger during autumn and winter is the dried hydrangea. These blooms should be left growing until they are fading or past their best (see page 30).

Other ideas for the drying process include adding a little dye to the glycerine to strengthen colour when needed. Another tip is to give some of the shorter flowers and leaves false wire stems before drying as they will be too brittle to handle later.

Inserting a piece of wire in the shape of a crook into the centre of a flower.

It is easier and more effective to arrange dried flowers in small bunches. If necessary, add a toothpick for support and bind the stem with fine wire, using the end to pierce the floral foam. Florist's tape (on the left) is also useful for binding, although ordinary sticky tape will do.

Seasonal Tips

Every season brings fresh ideas for flower arrangers. In these final pages, I offer a few extra suggestions for making the most of each time of the year.

Spring

The advent of spring flowers is a delight after the sparse choice of flowers in winter. The small delicate flowers that grow close to the ground so as to be sheltered from the wind, such as primroses, violets and snowdrops, can be arranged in dainty glass containers or china bowls. The slightly longer-stemmed grape hyacinths, scillas and dwarf narcissi, arranged in a blue and white china tea cup and saucer and placed on a coffee or small side table, make a fresh-looking display.

DAFFODILS AND NARCISSI

Yellow is the predominant colour among spring flowers, the most common being the daffodil and narcissi. These should be bought or picked when they are in bud as they open very quickly once they are placed in a warm environment but do not pick the buds until some yellow is showing as totally green buds will not open once they are picked.

There are many different varieties of daffodils and narcissi that range in size as well as colour. Try to include some of the blooms that have a different-coloured centre cup to the outer petals in your arrangements. *Narcissus* 'Armada' with an orange cup and yellow petals, 'Tudor Minstrel' with a yellow frill-edged cup and over-lapping white petals and *Narcissus* 'Actaea' with white petals and small yellow cups edged with dark crimson are just some of the many to choose from. These long-stemmed flowers look splendid when arranged formally with purple irises and bronze tulips.

An all-yellow arrangement can look just as fine using all-yellow daffodils, yellow irises, yellow tulips and long, thin delicate sprays of jasmine or forsythia and pussy willow.

SPRING BLOSSOMS

Spring produces some of the most attractive blossoms and flowering shrubs and these add beauty to any home (see pages 18–19). You will only need a few pieces of heavily laden blossom as too much will detract from the natural grace of their arched branches. Blossom is picked when it is in tight bud as it opens rapidly once it is brought inside.

The prunus family offers the greatest variety of ornamental blossom, including cherry, almond, plum and peach, which all flower at different times during the early spring months. One of my favourite spring-flowering shrubs is corylopsis with its racemes of pale yellow flowers which appear in March and April.

Three curved sprays of this sweet-smelling shrub are enough when placed in a tall container or bottle. Other flowering shrubs are azaleas and *Philadelphus*, often called mock orange.

There are so many different spring flowers and shrubs that it is impossible to mention them all but by experimenting with cultivated as well as wild flowers, your arrangements should be a delight both to you and to all who see them.

Yellow spring flowers in a simple but contrasting blue and white jug.

Summer

In summer there is an abundance of flowers to choose from: delphiniums, larkspur, Canterbury bells, godetias, carnations and spikes of gladioli but perhaps the most beautiful summer-flowering bloom is the rose.

SUMMER ROSES

Probably no other flower has been endowed with as many legends as the rose. Mythology tells us that its birth coincided with that of Venus, the goddess of love, so in the language of flowers, the rose is the symbol of love.

Almost everyone is drawn to roses and certainly, no flower is more delightful when arranged in the home. Colour and variety are a matter of personal choice but the range is so wide that there is hardly an occasion when the appropriate rose is not available.

Always remember to cut roses before they are fully open: so many people leave the blooms on the bushes until they are almost fully blown, then wonder why they do not last well indoors. Cut your roses above a leaf joint whenever possible, remove the lower leaves and scrape off the thorns which will be below the waterline of your container. Split the stem ends with a knife, or scissors, and stand the stems in deep water for several hours to condition them.

Use non-patterned, simple containers so as not to detract from the beauty of the flowers. There is no doubt that the ideal container for roses is a bowl of one sort or another, for here they can be arranged in masses, with foliage, so that they look as natural as possible. A pin-holder can be placed in the base of a modern bowl and filled with crumpled wire netting to give added support to the stems.

Roses grow in many different varieties. The Floribunda Roses have single, semi-double or double flowers in clusters and it is best to clip out some of the more open heads to avoid a thick and heavy arrangement. The flower heads which have been removed can be used in wine glasses or floated on the top of a small glass bowl filled with water. The Hybrid Tea Rose and the Garnett type of rose are very good varieties for cutting as they last well in water. White roses such as 'Iceberg' are ideal for weddings and the pink varieties 'Dearest' and 'Queen Elizabeth' are perfect for home decorations. Yellow and orange-coloured roses are perhaps the best for parties and receptions held in the evenings as they show up well. But, for those who wish to be a little different there are many unusual and attractive colours to choose from, such as mauve, silver, brown and bicolours – you just need to watch the catalogues.

Summer roses, everyone's favourite, here mixed with gypsophila and hosta leaves.

In addition to roses, I love peonies of all colours and varieties, also the peach-coloured digitalis. Then lilies are important for many summer decorations, particularly when grouped with fennel, as well as the euphorbias. Few of us can be without *Alchemilla mollis*, with its pale green feathery flowers, or sweet peas and aquilegias, so reminiscent of cottage gardens.

Summer is a high season for flowers so you need never be without, especially if you sowed the seeds of annual flowers in early summer, for they will now be showing their colours.

Autumn

Early autumn sees an end to the wealth of bright-coloured summer flowers and the garden and countryside take on a golden appearance. Flowers are no longer plentiful but there are still a few dahlias and crinums to be found and, of course, the ever-faithful chrysanthemum to add extra colour to an arrangement of autumn foliage.

CHRYSANTHEMUMS

The bronze, yellow and deep pink colours of chrysanthemums harmonize well with autumn leaves and, by using different shaped flowers, exciting decorations can be achieved (see pages 40–41). The light bronze, thread-petalled 'Bronze Rayonnate' and the anemone-centred 'Catena' are both a joy to behold. The single-flowering 'Mason's Bronze' with its daisy-like yellow centres is ideal for arranging with bright yellow and flame-coloured berries. The yellow spray type, such as 'Yellow Marble' and the spider type, like 'Golden Crystal', will look especially fine if arranged with some dark, shiny green-yellow leaves, such as *Elaeagnus pungens* 'Maculata', rhododendron or golden privet (*Ligustrum*).

FOLIAGE

A charming autumnal arrangement can be created with russet-coloured leaves from the garden and countryside. The small leaves of tellima, an evergreen perennial, turn a rich copper bronze in autumn and *Sorbus sargentiana* turns bright red. *Fothergilla monticola*, with orange, red and yellow-tinted leaves, and the autumn foliage of viburnum can be used to great effect.

Fatsia japonica, another good stand-by, especially for modern designs.

Euonymus 'Silver Queen', one of my favourite evergreen shrubs.

SEEDS

There are several different plants that produce bright red and orange seeds in autumn, which can be incorporated into foliage. The seedpods of *Iris foetidissima* split open and curve outwards, to reveal scarlet-coloured seeds. The paper-like, lantern-shaped seedheads of

the Chinese lantern (*Physalis alkekengi*) add a bright splash of orange to any decoration. For a darker orange-red, use the variety of Chinese lantern called 'Franchetii'. The twining branches of *Celastrus orbiculatus* not only have attractive autumn leaves but, when the leaves fall, clusters of bright scarlet fruit are left behind. These branches can be arranged on their own into an elegant design.

FRUIT

Fruit can add colour as well as form to a foliage arrangement. For a centre-table decoration, a bowl of green apples, into which stems of glossy *Choisya ternata* (Mexican orange) or *Viburnum tinus* are tucked, makes an original table display. The apples can rest on a block of water-soaked foam which has been wrapped in plastic, as fruit should never be allowed to lie directly on wet foam. The stems of the leaves are inserted into the foam between the apples. In my opinion, there is nothing more lovely in late summer or early autumn than a grouping of pale green grapes and some peaches with autumn-coloured foliage. As some fruit is shiny and some has a dull surface, to show each to their best advantage, place dull fruit against shiny leaves and shiny fruit against dull leaves.

Winter

Winter is the time of year when flowers are at their most expensive and it is then that flowering shrubs and evergreen foliage can be used to their best advantage.

EVERGREEN LEAVES

An arrangement of leaves can have just a few flowers added for extra colour; although if you study the many forms, shapes, sizes and colours of leaves you can create the most interesting decorations using foliage only. Follow the same principles of design as for other arrangements, using the taller pointed leaves for outline and placing the larger rosette types in the centre. Fill in with less important leaves.

If you are making a modern design, place the tall pointed leaves on a pin-holder to give height and insert some broader and shorter ones lower down as transition. Add a few larger, rounder, more dominant leaves at the base of the arrangement for focal interest.

BERRIES

Some shrubs have bright-coloured berries throughout the winter and some even bear flowers. These can be arranged with leaves or on their own. The berberis family contains many berried varieties, the scarlet berries of *Berberis thunbergii* and the coral-red fruit of *Berberis × rubrostilla* are just two examples of many. *Cotoneaster* 'Cornubia', a semi-evergreen shrub, has branches which are

Choisya ternata, *always useful for filling in.*

heavily laden with fruit. The snowberry (*Symphoricarpos*) bears white berries on its arched branches from autumn onwards.

SHRUBS

Perhaps the finest winter-flowering shrub is mahonia. This dark green, shiny-leaved shrub has bright yellow clusters of flowers during the winter months. *Mahonia* 'Charity' has long spikes of sweet-smelling, deep yellow flowers and *Mahonia bealei* has lemon-yellow flowers.

Winter-flowering jasmine can be arranged with variegated leaves to make a light and delicate arrangement and sprays of golden privet (*Ligustrum*) can form the background for yellow chrysanthemums, creating a bright arrangement during the long winter months.

Remember that whatever plant material you are using, it must be conditioned before being arranged (see pages 76–78).

When cutting from evergreen shrubs, it is better to cut from the back and underneath as this is usually where the interesting curves are to be found. You can cut from the centre of the shrub which will thin it out, but always cut just above an outward-pointing bud.

Floral foam can be used to support the leaves in the container but it is preferable to place the leaves in clear water, using wire netting to hold the stems in place.

Here is a list of some more of my favourite evergreen leaves which I would not be without:

Mahonia aquifolium	*Skimmia*
Viburnum tinus	*Camellia*
Elaeagnus pungens 'Maculata'	*Ribes*
Ligustrum (privet)	*Lonicera*
Aucuba japonica (spotted laurel)	*Rhododendron*

IVY AND HOUSEPLANTS

One must not forget the different ivies and vigorously growing houseplants, which will not suffer if some of their leaves are removed when other foliage is scarce. You can always cut from the green climber *Cissus antartica*, commonly known as the kangeroo vine, and *Tradescantia fluminensis* 'Quicksilver' will constantly give variegated trails. If a burst of strap-like leaves are required for central interest, then try *Chlorophytum* (spider plant).

Index

The publishers and author would like to thank *Garden News*, Rod Sloane and Jon Whitbourne for their help with the photographs.